ANIMALS ON THE BRINK

Orangutans

Patricia Miller-Schroeder

www.av2books.com

MEDIA ENHANCED BOOKS
AV²
BY WEIGL™
ADDED VALUE • AUDIO VISUAL

Go to **www.av2books.com**, and enter this book's unique code.

BOOK CODE

B 2 1 1 1 6 2

AV² by Weigl brings you media enhanced books that support active learning.

AV² provides enriched content that supplements and complements this book. Weigl's AV² books strive to create inspired learning and engage young minds in a total learning experience.

Your AV² Media Enhanced books come alive with...

Audio
Listen to sections of the book read aloud.

Key Words
Study vocabulary, and complete a matching word activity.

Video
Watch informative video clips.

Quizzes
Test your knowledge.

Embedded Weblinks
Gain additional information for research.

Slide Show
View images and captions, and prepare a presentation.

Try This!
Complete activities and hands-on experiments.

... and much, much more!

Published by AV² by Weigl
350 5th Avenue, 59th Floor
New York, NY 10118
Websites: www.av2books.com   www.weigl.com

Library of Congress Control Number: 2013953040

ISBN 978-1-4896-0572-6 (hardcover)
ISBN 978-1-4896-0573-3 (softcover)
ISBN 978-1-4896-0574-0 (single-user eBook)
ISBN 978-1-4896-0575-7 (multi-user eBook)

Printed in the United States of America in North Mankato, Minnesota
1 2 3 4 5 6 7 8 9 17 16 15 14 13

122013
WEP301113

Project Coordinator Aaron Carr
Design Mandy Christiansen

Every reasonable effort has been made to trace ownership and to obtain permission to reprint copyright material. The publishers would be pleased to have any errors or omissions brought to their attention so that they may be corrected in subsequent printings.

Photo Credits
Weigl acknowledges Getty Images as its primary photo supplier for this title.

Contents

AV² Book Code 2

The Orangutan 4

Features 6

Classification 8

Special Adaptations 10

Groups 12

Communication 14

Body Language 16

Mating and Birth 18

Baby Orangutans 20

Development 22

Habitat 24

Range 26

Place on the Planet 28

Diet 30

The Food Cycle 32

Competition 34

Orangutans with Other Animals 36

Folklore 38

Status 40

Saving the Orangutan 42

Back from the Brink 44

Activity 45

Quiz 46

Key Words/Index 47

Log on to www.av2books.com 48

Take a Stand

Debate · Research

How to take a stand on an issue **5**

Should humans be allowed to keep baby orangutans? **17**

Can people help orangutans by refusing to buy items made with palm oil? **29**

Should orangutans that have been rescued from captivity be released back into their natural habitat? **33**

The Orangutan

Deep in the rainforests of Indonesia and Malaysia lives a mysterious animal with flowing, flame-red hair. The people on the islands of Borneo and Sumatra gave this creature the name orangutan, which means "person of the forest." Orangutans are the only great apes living in nature in Asia, and they were the last great apes to be studied by Western scientists. Even today, orangutans are the least understood of all types of apes.

In this book you will discover why orangutans are the most solitary of all the apes. You will learn how this heavy animal moves easily through treetops and why an orangutan is rarely found on the ground. You will discover the most important lessons a young orangutan has to learn. Turn the pages to enter the fascinating world of the red apes of Asia.

Adult male orangutans usually try to keep their distance from one another.

Orangutans are peaceful by nature, unless they have to defend themselves.

How to Take a Stand on an Issue

Research is important to the study of any scientific field. When scientists choose a subject to study, they must conduct research to ensure they have a thorough understanding of the topic. They ask questions about the subject and then search for answers. Sometimes, however, there is no clear answer to a question. In these cases, scientists must use the information they have to form a hypothesis, or theory. They must take a stand on one side of an issue or the other. Follow the process below for each Take a Stand section in this book to determine where you stand on these issues.

1. **What is the Issue?**
   a. Determine a research subject, and form a general question about the subject.

2. **Form a Hypothesis**
   a. Search at the library and online for sources of information on the subject.
   b. Conduct basic research on the subject to narrow down the general question.
   c. Form a hypothesis on the subject based on research to this point.
   d. Make predictions based on the hypothesis. What are the expected results?

3. **Research the Issue**
   a. Conduct extensive research using a variety of sources, including books, scientific journals, and reliable websites.
   b. Collect data on the issue and take notes on all information gathered from research.
   c. Draw conclusions based on the information collected.

4. **Conclusion**
   a. Explain the research findings.
   b. Was the hypothesis proved or disproved?

Observing
Orangutans

Orangutans in captivity
have learned to work
zippers, use computer
keyboards, and even unlock
their cage doors.

Orangutans have been seen using
sticks to determine how deep water is.

Features

Orangutans have several striking features and abilities. They communicate with sounds and gestures, much the way that people do. These great apes can walk upright on two legs and handle objects with their hands. Their **genetic makeup** is part of the reason that orangutans are capable of such things.

These great apes have a pattern of genes that is similar in a number of ways to that of humans. In fact, most of the **DNA** of humans and orangutans is the same. In the scientific classification of animals, orangutans are considered **primates**, a group of animals known in part for its use of tools, social behaviors, and ability to plan.

Orangutans have adapted to their forest environment. They have become good problem solvers. For example, some of them have learned to look for cracks on prickly fruit so they can insert sticks and pry out the tasty insides. The rainforests where orangutans have lived for thousands of years present many challenges to their survival.

Today, two **species** of orangutan are living on two islands in Asia. Although they once ranged across the rainforests of Southeast Asia, orangutans are now found only on Sumatra and Borneo. A different species lives on each island. Both species are similar, but they have slightly different characteristics. The Sumatran orangutan, for example, tends to have lighter coloring, but the hair of the orangutans in Borneo tends to be shinier. Both males and females in Sumatra grow beards as they age. In Borneo, however, it is usually just the male orangutans that develop beards.

Male orangutans can weigh 250 pounds (115 kilograms) or more. Females are less than half that weight, at about 110 pounds (50 kg). Adult males have an arm span that stretches to 8 feet (2.5 meters). An average male stands 4.5 feet (1.8 m) tall. Females are shorter and have a smaller arm span. The orangutans from Borneo are heavier and larger than the ones from Sumatra.

Classification

The **order** of animals known as primates includes humans, apes, monkeys, and prosimians. The prosimians are a group of small primates that includes lemurs. Primates are alike in basic ways, such as the size of their brains relative to their bodies. Scientists divide this order of animals into other, smaller groupings based on certain characteristics. For example, the primates can be divided into 11 families. Monkeys are part of the family Tarsiidae.

Orangutans are in the family Homindae, also known as the great apes. Along with chimpanzees, bonobos, and gorillas, orangutans are one of only four types of great apes left in the world. They are known as "great" because of their size. A gorilla, the largest primate found in Africa, can weigh more than 400 pounds (180 kg). The orangutan is the largest primate in Asia. By comparison, its smallest primate relative, the mouse lemur, weighs 2 ounces (60 grams). Apes do not have tails, as do many other primates. Compared with others in their order, apes have broader chests and tend to stand more upright.

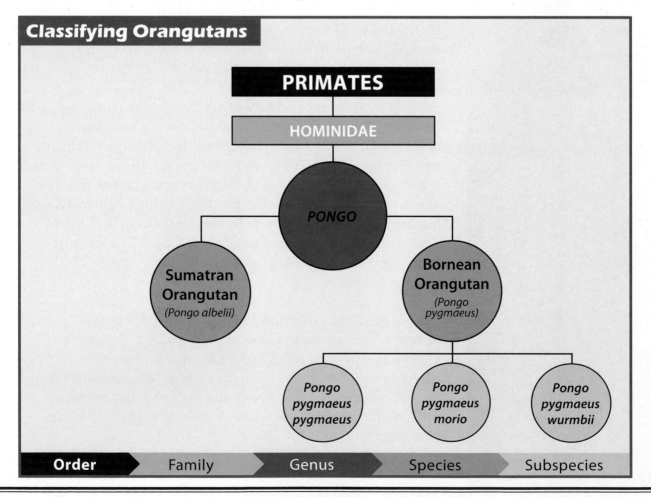

Classifying Orangutans

PRIMATES

HOMINIDAE

PONGO

Sumatran Orangutan
(Pongo albelii)

Bornean Orangutan
(Pongo pygmaeus)

Pongo pygmaeus pygmaeus

Pongo pygmaeus morio

Pongo pygmaeus wurmbii

Order → Family → Genus → Species → Subspecies

Hair length and thickness varies in orangutans. Some have full, flowing coats, while others have thinner coats with patches of skin showing through.

Among orangutan males, the Sumatran orangutans are leaner and usually have oval faces. Often, they have long golden-colored mustaches and beards.

Scientists divide Bornean orangutans into three subspecies, or types, based on where the apes live. The Central Bornean orangutans are the largest of the three.

Special Adaptations

Orangutans have many special features that help them survive in the rainforests of Southeast Asia. For example, their hands are well adapted to life in the trees. Their long, curved fingers can grasp tightly onto branches when they move through treetops.

Teeth

Like humans, orangutans have 32 permanent teeth, but orangutan teeth are larger and stronger. The large back teeth can crush hard plant material and crack hard nutshells. The sharp **canine** teeth can bite through tough fruit skins. Males have longer canine teeth that they use for fighting or threatening other animals.

Hands

An orangutan's hands are not as useful as those of other primates for grasping small items, but these great apes can still carry and make use of objects. Orangutans use their hands to pick fruit and build nests in the trees. Like humans, orangutans have tiny raised fingerprints on the tips of their fingers. These ridges help them feel and hang on to things.

Eyes

Orangutans can see in color and have binocular vision. This means that both eyes look straight ahead but see their surroundings from a slightly different angle. Orangutans depend on their eyesight to help them judge distances and depth. This is essential when traveling through the trees. Their color vision also helps them locate the fruit and other plants they need to eat.

Arms and Legs

Orangutans are the most **arboreal** of the great apes. They can move gracefully and safely through the swaying branches of trees, 100 feet (30 m) above the forest floor. Their long arms, short legs, and hook-like hands and feet allow even large orangutans to swing through trees. This ability is important because a fall can cause broken bones, serious injuries, or death.

Feet

An orangutan's feet resemble its hands in many ways. Both help the orangutan to hang onto branches while traveling. An orangutan's toes are long and **prehensile**. This is a good safety feature for an animal that spends most of its time in the treetops.

Observing
Orangutans

Orangutans will sometimes travel together for a short period of time, but only in areas where fruit is plentiful. In these cases, only a few orangutans take part in the food search, and they remain together for just a few days.

The most common grouping of orangutans is a mother and her children.

Groups

Orangutans live in very different social groups from the other great apes. While chimpanzees, bonobos, and gorillas usually live with several group members, orangutans spend much of their lives alone. This solitary lifestyle is an adaptation to the environment in which orangutans live.

Fruit, their main source of food, is widely scattered in the rainforest. It is often available only during certain seasons. This means large animals such as orangutans must travel great distances to find enough food to eat. Animals living and traveling by themselves have a better chance of finding food and surviving. That is why orangutans in nature do not form long-lasting social groups.

The only orangutans that stay together for long periods of time are mothers and their offspring. Groups may form at other times for brief periods, however. This sometimes happens when females and their young meet at a large source of food, such as a fruit-bearing tree. In these cases, the females usually feed together peacefully while the young play in groups.

When female orangutans are ready to mate, they often form a partnership with a male for a few hours or perhaps a few days. Sometimes, female orangutans will seek out certain males with whom they are familiar. They may do this when they are ready to mate or when an unfamiliar male is bothering them.

A **dominant** male will try to keep other mature males away from any potential mates. He may threaten or attack another male that comes near. These are unfriendly meetings and last only as long as it takes for one male to chase the other away. As is true with various kinds of animals, the older, powerful males are more dominant than younger or smaller males.

Young orangutans will play together if given the chance.

Observing Orangutans

If an orangutan is annoyed, it may make a sound that is a combination of a kiss and a squeak. The animal tightens its lips and then makes a squeaky smack.

An orangutan uses a variety of noises to communicate rather than wordlike sounds.

Communication

Orangutans are intelligent animals that have a variety of ways to communicate with each other. Among the great apes, orangutans are the least vocal, but they still send messages to one another with their sounds, body language, and displays. Orangutans in captivity have even been taught to communicate with humans through sign language.

The most impressive sound among orangutans is the males' long call. This deep, booming call resembles the roar of a lion. The long call can be so forceful that it carries for 0.5 miles (0.8 km) or more through the forest. It starts with a low rumbling, which becomes a loud groaning and finally a terrific booming roar that ends in more rumbles and sighs.

Male orangutans have large throat pouches, which contain an air sac that amplifies sound, or makes it louder. When rival adult males hear the long call of a dominant male, they tend to move away from the source. They heed the call as a warning unless they want to challenge the other male's dominance.

Adult male orangutans try to attract females by bellowing loudly and sometimes by breaking and throwing branches. Some females move toward the sound, especially if they are ready to mate. Females are more likely to move toward a calling male if they know him. Sometimes, females will move away from the calling male. They tend to behave this way if he is a stranger or they are not looking for a mate.

Orangutans make various sounds in response to their surroundings and one another. These include barks, moans, screams, squeaks, and whimpers. These sounds are more likely to come from young orangutans that are playing or are frightened. Young orangutans like to be tickled when playing, and they then make sounds that resemble human laughter.

Although orangutans spend much of their adult lives alone, they share behaviors that are important in communicating. Certain signals and behaviors known as body language allow the solitary adults to understand one another when they spend time with other orangutans. They will often gesture to one another, rather than make sounds, to get their meaning across.

Dominance Stare

When males meet, they stand stiffly to make themselves look as large as possible. Mature males will stare at each other and inflate their throat pouches to see if the other will back down. They sometimes open their mouths to show their large canine teeth, or they pinch their lips tightly together.

Threat Response

Young orangutans learn body language behaviors by watching their mothers. For example, when orangutans feel threatened by another animal, they will shake trees and break branches to try to scare off the animal.

Clowning

Young orangutans spend part of their time clowning around. In the trees, they will hang upside down and make faces. On the ground, they will perform back rolls. Sometimes, they make funny blowing sounds, called "raspberries," with their mouths.

Begging

Hungry young orangutans ask for food by holding a hand out. They may also cup a hand under the chin of their mothers. If the mother is holding food, the youngster may move his or her eyes back and forth from the food to the mother's eyes.

Should humans be allowed to keep baby orangutans?

Humans serve as caretakers for many types of animals, such as dogs, cats, birds, and fish, that families keep as pets. Farm animals help provide people with food, transportation, and even energy for performing work. Can orangutans be pets and helpers, too?

FOR

1. Baby orangutans can be taught to drink from a bottle and wear diapers. These primates are smart animals that might benefit from human care, if placed in the right setting.
2. Orangutans are in danger of dying out, so it makes sense to allow people to try to raise them, keep them healthy, and help keep their species alive on the planet.

AGAINST

1. Baby orangutans are small and needy, but these cute babies grow into very large apes. Many people find the growing animals too hard to manage.
2. Orangutans may seem like people in some limited respects, but they have their own special needs and are built to live in trees. They experience stress in captivity. Confining these animals to a human lifestyle is just not right.

Observing Orangutans

Most orangutans build their nests high in the trees, between 40 and 60 feet (12 and 18 m) above the ground. The nests are sturdy and can measure 3 feet (1 m) or more in diameter.

Orangutans use thick branches to form the frame of the nest and piles of thin branches as a mattress.

Mating and Birth

The **gestation period** for orangutans is about 250 days. An orangutan infant is usually born in one of its mother's nests. Orangutans tend to build a new nest each night because they must travel a great deal while looking for food. They may also build one or two nests during the day for napping or resting while feeding. Orangutans build their nests by bending and weaving branches and leafy plants into a basket shape.

An adult female orangutan may give birth to only two to four infants in her lifetime. Usually, only one infant is born at a time, but twins have been born in captivity. Births can occur at any time of the year. The mother orangutan cares for her infant for many years. She may not give birth again until her youngster is about 8 years old.

The baby orangutan is dependent on the mother for food, transportation, and important life lessons, such as how to build a nest. Shortly after giving birth, the mother cleans the infant. The little orangutan then begins to nurse on its mother's warm milk. This is the start of the longest and closest relationship in an orangutan's life.

The mother orangutan carries her infant with her for several years. She keeps the baby safe and warm by cradling it to her body. During an orangutan's childhood, its mother is its only guardian and teacher. Adult male orangutans take little part in caring for infants or juvenile orangutans in nature.

From an Expert

*"Orangutans share about 97 percent of their genetic material with humans. If wild orangutans go **extinct**, we will have lost not only a unique and engaging species but also a cousin."*
Biruté Mary Galdikas

Biruté Mary Galdikas has studied orangutans in Borneo since 1971 and is considered the foremost authority on the subject. She established the first rehabilitation center for orangutans. Galdikas is also the co-founder and president of the Orangutan Foundation International, which works to protect orangutans.

Baby Orangutans

An orangutan weighs only about 4 pounds (1.8 kg) at birth. Its body is covered with red hair, which may stand straight up on its head. Pink patches of skin circle its eyes and mouth.

An infant orangutan has grasping hands and feet that cling tightly to the hair on its mother's chest and belly. The mother supports the infant with one of her hands or knees while she is moving around. The mother orangutan provides the milk that is the infant's main food for its first year of life.

By 1 year of age, the infant weighs about 15 pounds (6.8 kg). The baby is becoming stronger and more coordinated. By this time, the growing orangutan can ride easily on its mother's abdomen, clinging to her hair. The baby also starts tasting bits of plant food by this age. The mother teaches the baby which foods are safe to eat.

Young orangutans continue to nurse long after they are eating plant food. Some may nurse until they are 5 or 6 years old if their mothers allow them, but most orangutans have gained some independence by the age of 3. They try new foods and practice nest building, though they still share their mother's nest at night.

Some young orangutans are **weaned** by the time they are 3 years old. They can move around in the trees at this age. They practice climbing with their mother's help.

Like a human infant, a baby orangutan will cry when hungry.

Observing
Orangutans

To walk, a baby orangutan must learn to move on two feet and support its movement with the sides of its palms.

Orangutans have the longest childhood of any primates except humans. The survival skills the mother teaches are complex and take time to learn.

Observing Orangutans

The many swaying trees, shrubs, and vines in the rainforest provide an adventure playground. Young orangutans are good acrobats.

An orangutan can use both hands and feet equally well for climbing and other tasks.

Development

A mother orangutan helps her offspring learn to make nests. She may bend some branches for them or make a bridge over a large open space in the trees with her body. As they get older, young orangutans explore farther away from their mothers but still depend on them for support.

Juveniles like rough play with other youngsters when they meet them in their travels. Play is an important activity for all young primates. Young orangutans sometimes play in their nests and often practice building nests as part of their play. Many will pile branches over their heads. They also practice finding and trying new foods by imitating their mothers. Their play helps them learn new skills and test their strength and agility. The young spend much of their time climbing trees and swinging from branch to branch. They sometimes hang by their feet and try somersaulting.

A young female's childhood ends by 7 or 8 years of age, when her mother has another small infant. At this age, she remains close to her mother and learns how to be a mother herself. By 9 or 10 years old, she may live on her own but see her mother at times.

The male orangutan's childhood is also coming to an end by 7 or 8 years of age. After his mother gives birth to her next child, a young male orangutan gradually travels farther away. He may meet up with other juveniles and see or visit his mother from time to time.

By the time she is 15 years old, a female orangutan weighs about 70 to 80 pounds (31 to 36 kg) and is ready to mate. Male orangutans are slower to mature than females. By the age of 18, many males are fully mature, with throat and cheek pouches and longer, darker hair. Some males may take even longer to mature. Most males will wander through the forest until they locate a home range for themselves and find females with which to mate.

The long relationship between orangutan babies and mothers is rare among mammals.

Habitat

Orangutans thrive in tropical forests. They are found in nature in lowland rainforests and peat-swamp forests, where the trees provide food, shelter, and even drinking water. Orangutans drink water by dipping their hands in hollow places on tree branches where rain collects. Sometimes, they lick water drops off leaves. When water is hard to find, the orangutans will chew leaves to form a kind of sponge. They then insert their leafy sponges into holes in trees to get at the moisture inside.

These great apes spend 95 percent of their time 20 to 100 feet (6 to 30 m) above the forest floor. They rarely come down to the ground unless travel in the trees is difficult or they need to find food. The forest floor may be flooded during the rainy season of the year.

Organizing the Tropical Forest

Earth is home to millions of different **organisms**, all of which have specific survival needs. These organisms rely on their environment, or the place where they live, for their survival. All plants and animals have relationships with their environment. They interact with the environment itself, as well as the other plants and animals within the environment. These interactions create **ecosystems**.

Ecosystems can be broken down into levels of organization. These levels range from a single plant or animal to many species of plants and animals living together in an area.

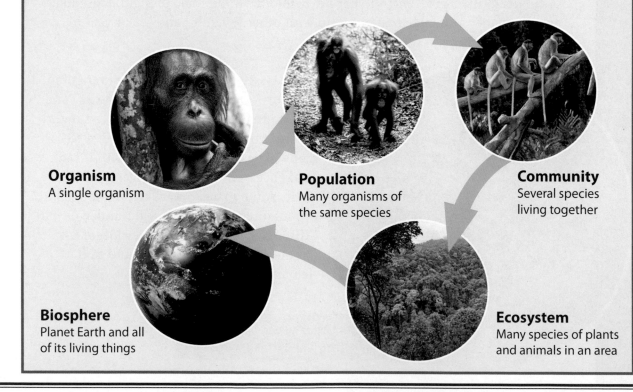

Organism
A single organism

Population
Many organisms of the same species

Community
Several species living together

Biosphere
Planet Earth and all of its living things

Ecosystem
Many species of plants and animals in an area

In their natural habitat, orangutans live for 35 to 50 years.

Observing Orangutans

The arms of orangutans are made for swinging in trees. Their arms are 1.5 times longer than their legs.

Sometimes, an orangutan shifts its weight back and forth in order to make a tree move, or sway. When the swaying tree comes close enough to the next tree, the orangutan swings over.

Range

In order to share the food resources of the forest, orangutans each have their own **home range**. A dominant male has a home range of at least 3.1 square miles (8 square kilometers). Females and young or less powerful males will often have home ranges of about 0.6 square miles (1.5 sq. km). Home ranges may overlap loosely, as orangutans travel around looking for food. Several females may have home ranges that fall inside a larger one belonging to a dominant male. Adolescent males do not have a fixed range but wander in search of a home range of their own.

How widely orangutans space themselves depends on the type of habitat they live in. Swamp forests have more resources, so they can support about eight orangutans per 0.7 square mile (1 sq. km). In hilly regions, there is less food, so only about five orangutans can live in an area of the same size. Adult male orangutans may travel great distances in search of food. The older males sometimes descend to the ground to feed and travel. They may disappear from part of their home range for years at a time before returning to the same area.

Each orangutan must carry a mental map of its home range, since the locations of food sources are so widely spaced. Many trees bear fruit at different times. The orangutans must know exactly when to travel to these trees. They must also be able to tell fruit trees apart from the dozens of other trees in their range. Each orangutan learns these things from its mother during its childhood.

From an Expert

"We assume that the critical factor for using tools is the ability to learn it from others. Everybody is using tools and everybody can observe it, so it is a social behavior . . . but, say the orangutan population is reduced, or goes extinct. Then this behavior will die out. You can reintroduce orangutans into the wild, but not a culture."
Carel van Schaik

Carel van Schaik teaches at the University of Zurich in Switzerland. He was the first scientist to document tool use by orangutans hunting for food in the swampy Gunung Leuser National Park in Sumatra.

Place on the Planet

Orangutans have their own special place on the planet, the rainforests of the large islands of Borneo and Sumatra. Each of these natural habitats has a variety of plants, including many fruit trees. While orangutans eat various parts of many plants, their main food item is fruit. The various types of rainforest fruit trees, which bear fruit at different times, provide food for the orangutans all year.

Where Orangutans Live

South
China
Sea

MALAYSIA

Borneo

Sumatra

Sulawesi

INDONESIA

Java

LEGEND
Malaysia
Indonesia
Orangutan
Habitats

N

0   500 Miles

0   500 Kilometers

In Sumatra, orangutans live only in the northern part of the island. The forests there are in hilly areas 0 to 3,280 feet (0 to 1,000 m) above sea level. In Borneo, orangutans live in Kalimantan, the region of the island that is part of Indonesia. They also live in Sarawak and Sabah, which are parts of the country of Malaysia. The apes' habitat on Borneo is lowland forest or swamp forest about 100 to 1,665 feet (30 to 500 m) above sea level.

Orangutans are **diurnal.** They wake up shortly before sunrise and go to sleep at sunset. When they wake up, they often visit the trees they were feeding from the day before. Then, they move on in search of new food sources. Orangutans spend about 60 percent of their day searching for food and eating. These great apes travel from one part of their range to another depending on what fruit is available or where other food might be found.

Orangutans would rather avoid each other than fight. The habitat they live in, however, is becoming smaller. In some areas, trees are being cut down for lumber. Sometimes, people set fire to areas of the forest to clear the land for farming or other activities. Orangutans are being forced to survive in smaller and smaller areas. This causes competition among orangutans for a shrinking food supply. Some of them are dying from lack of food as a result of these changes.

Take a Stand

Debate · *Research*

Can people help orangutans by refusing to buy items made with palm oil?

Palm oil, made from palm fruit, is an ingredient in many products, from baked goods to cosmetics. In Borneo and Sumatra, orangutans die when people cut and burn the rainforest to make way for palm fruit plantations.

FOR

1. By refusing to buy products with palm oil, people can reduce the amount of land that is cleared to raise palm fruit. The companies will switch to using some other kind of oil.
2. Palm oil is often used in sugary snacks. By eating more healthful foods instead, people can cut the demand for these foods and help save the orangutan's habitat.

AGAINST

1. Some palm fruit is raised in a way that does not hurt the environment or animals. If people stop buying things made with palm oil, they might be hurting some companies for no reason.
2. A more direct way to help orangutans would be to help finance the groups that work to save them. People can also help groups that try to protect the land where orangutans live.

Diet

Depending on what food is available, orangutans can be omnivores, which means that they eat both plants and animals. Most of the time, however, orangutans are herbivores. This means that they eat just plants. About 60 percent of the plant food they eat is fruit. Animals that eat mainly fruit are also known as frugivores.

Orangutans are **mammals**. They are the largest mammals to eat a mainly fruit diet. Some of the fruits eaten by orangutans are strangling fig, rambutan, jackfruit, lansat, mangostein, breadfruit, wild plum, and durian. Durian is the size of a football. It is said to taste like cheesy custard and smell like rotten eggs.

Orangutans also eat flowers, young leaves and shoots, bamboo, nuts, and bark. Researchers have counted more than 400 different plant species that orangutans use as food sources. Once they locate food, they must find ways of getting it. The tasty parts of the fruits and plants they eat are often hidden beneath prickly or hard surfaces.

Orangutans add animal protein to their diet when they can get it. They will eat birds' eggs and insects such as ants, termites, and caterpillars. In addition, they may eat small animals such as lizards and young squirrels. If an orangutan finds a bees' nest, he or she will often eat the honey inside.

The orangutan's favorite food is the fruit of the durian tree.

Observing Orangutans

An orangutan's body does not digest all the parts of every plant it eats. To help with digestion, an orangutan will sometimes eat soil.

The type of food energy orangutans get from leaves helps them stay active throughout the day.

The Food Cycle

A food cycle shows how energy in the form of food is passed from one living thing to another. Orangutans survive by eating mainly plant food. As orangutans move through the forest searching for food, they affect the lives of other living things. The diagram below shows the flow of energy from one living thing to the next through a **food web**.

Primary Consumers

Orangutans eat many types of plant foods, such as figs, wild plums, durian, bamboo, flowers, and nuts.

Secondary Consumers

Very rarely, **predators** such as the clouded leopard and Sumatran tiger take a young, old, or sick orangutan.

Parasites

The orangutan provides a home for parasites such as worms.

Omnivores

Besides plants, orangutans sometimes eat ants, termites, caterpillars, and other insects, as well as small **vertebrate** animals, such as lizards and squirrels.

Producers

In the rainforest, plants use sunlight and nutrients from the soil to produce food energy. Orangutans eat plants and play an important role in spreading seeds from one part of their habitat to another. Undigested seeds in orangutan droppings take root and grow into new fruit trees.

Decomposers

When an orangutan dies, decomposers found in the soil break down the body, adding nutrients to the soil.

Take a Stand

Debate • Research

Should orangutans that have been rescued from captivity be released back into their natural habitat?

Some people buy and sell infant orangutans illegally. Most often, these young orangutans were taken from their mothers' care too soon. Many of the infants are sick, weak, and frightened. When they are rescued, their future is uncertain.

FOR

1. The babies should be taken back to the rainforest. They deserve a chance to grow up and live in their natural home, swaying from one tree to another.
2. Orangutans are **endangered**. If rescued young orangutans are released in their natural habitat, they may be able to start new populations.

AGAINST

1. The stolen babies have not learned how to feed or care for themselves. Many young orangutans that are returned to nature do not survive. In some areas, only 50 percent survive.
2. Rescued orangutans may not fear humans or may even think they are humans. They could become pests and put themselves and humans in dangerous situations.

Observing Orangutans

Males develop large pouches of skin that hang below their chins. Their cheek pads and chin pouches make their faces appear larger and possibly more threatening to other male orangutans.

Young males avoid showing aggression toward one another.

Competition

Orangutans spend most of their time high in the treetops, searching for their next meal. As long as food is abundant, orangutans tend to leave one another, and the other fruit eaters in the forest, alone. Orangutans are not entirely peaceable, however. Sometimes, they compete with each other for mates. If food is scarce, they will even fight other animals for something to eat.

Scientists have discovered a **dominance hierarchy** among males. Weaker males will avoid contact with the large, dominant males. If two males do meet, they may exchange threats. Often, one male will back down. If neither one does, the threats may turn into a fight. The stronger male wins and remains dominant, with better access to food and females.

The hierarchy is so strong that the rate of maturity of younger males may slow down if a dominant male lives nearby. In this case, a male orangutan may not develop throat or cheek pouches or give long calls until he is 20 or more years old. Cheek pads indicate a male's maturity. Males are unable to attract females to mate with until they grow their cheek pads.

Females and especially younger orangutans tend to be more cooperative. When orangutans are very young, they turn to their mothers, or any older brothers or sisters who still live nearby, for playmates. Youngsters may scramble over their bodies or wrestle, tickle, tug, and bite them. Mothers are usually tolerant and may lift their young up onto a branch to help them practice climbing. As orangutans get a little older, they enjoy playing with other young orangutans they meet in the forest. This often happens when two or more mothers and their young meet at a large food source, such as a fruit tree.

From an Expert

"The orangutan is about to go extinct. I have [been] working with these fabulous and enchanting creatures and following them in their rainforest home, but I'm sorry to say you might not get that opportunity. We in Sumatra are doing as much as we can, but to be honest are fighting a losing battle."
Ian Singleton

Ian Singleton is the scientific director of the Sumatran Orangutan Conservation Programme in Medan, North Sumatra. This group returns rescued Sumatran orangutans into their natural habitat in Bukit Tigapuluh National Park.

Orangutans with Other Animals

O rangutans have shared the forests with many other animals for thousands of years. Other fruit-eating mammals, such as fruit bats and monkeys, use the same food sources as orangutans. So do birds such as hornbills. At a large fruit-bearing tree, there is usually enough to go around. There are also other fruit trees to be found.

Adult orangutans that are not weak or sick have little to fear from predators because of the apes' size and strength. Young orangutans who stay close to their mothers are often safe in the treetops, too. Today, however, there is one serious competitor causing a number of problems. Humans are competing with orangutans for the forest areas where the apes live. The rainforests that provide orangutans with their food and homes are being cut down. It is this competition from humans that has put orangutans at risk of extinction.

Orangutans share their habitat with other creatures, but all of them are finding their living space becoming smaller and smaller. As the forests shrink, orangutans come into competition with other fruit eaters more and more often. Many of these animals are rare or endangered. They include Sumatran rhinoceroses, gibbons, slow lorises, langurs, proboscis monkeys, sun bears, Asian elephants, and esturine crocodiles. The natural predators of the orangutan have been the clouded leopard and Sumatran tiger. Both are now very rare.

Fewer than 250 Sumatran rhinos survive in nature.

Observing Orangutans

There is no place for orangutans to go as the forests disappear on the islands where they live. The apes are often trapped in small areas of forest with open farmland, logging camps, or settlements blocking their movement into new regions.

The cheek pads on an adult male continue to grow during most of his life.

Folklore

The orangutan was first described by European explorers in the 17th and 18th centuries. The orangutan has had a long history with the people of Indonesia, however. Orangutan skulls dating back 35,000 years have been found in caves. Ancient orangutans were used either as food or as part of religious ceremonies by the prehistoric people who lived in Southeast Asia.

According to one legend, orangutans were bad people whom the gods had covered with red hair and banished to the forest for their wicked deeds. This legend may have contributed to the belief among early European explorers that orangutans were dangerous creatures, capable of kidnapping and harming humans. The apes' favorite victims were said to be young women. These false accounts even made their way into early natural history books.

In a legend of the Dayak people, who still live on Borneo, orangutans are ghosts that suddenly appear and disappear. The Dayak people treat orangutan skulls as sacred objects. Many of the Dayak people show their respect for the orangutan today by working to protect orangutans and the rainforest.

Museums around the world have exhibits that help people to learn facts about the great apes of Asia.

Myth	**VS**	Fact
 Orangutans are vicious and aggressive animals that can even kill crocodiles with their bare hands. They are likely to attack humans.		Orangutans are shy and would rather avoid other animals than fight. They are, however, very strong and will defend themselves or their young from humans or other animals if forced to do so.
Orangutans are dangerous animals that sometimes kidnap young women and carry them away into the treetops.		Orangutans are more likely to flee from humans than to kidnap them. A typical response to a strange human, woman or man, is for an orangutan to throw branches and make threat calls to discourage the person from getting too close. Then, the orangutan will move away through the treetops.
Orangutans are the least intelligent of the great apes. They do not communicate or use tools as other apes and humans do.		Orangutans have proved to be very intelligent. They are now known to make and use tools both in nature and in captivity. They also have many ways of communicating with other orangutans in nature.

Until scientists conducted field studies, observing orangutans in their natural habitat, people thought of orangutans as frightening animals.

Observing Orangutans

Sometimes, orangutans are hunted so that their parts can be sold as souvenirs to tourists.

It is not easy for orangutan populations to grow because these great apes give birth only once every six to seven years.

Status

Humans have pushed orangutans out of many parts of Indonesia and Malaysia where these animals used to live. The islands of Sumatra and Borneo have millions of people living on them. Many people think the forests where orangutans and other animals live are wasted space. Some people cut down the trees to sell for lumber or to plant crops, such as tea, which grows well in the climate of Sumatra and Borneo.

According to the World Wide Fund for Nature (WWF), the Bornean orangutan's habitat has shrunk by more than 55 percent in the past 20 years. The Sumatran orangutan is facing similar issues. Orangutans are now found only in areas of the northern part of the island of Sumatra.

As their habitat shrinks, orangutans raid crops to get food and come into conflict with people. Farmers may shoot apes that eat their crops. Sometimes, people also hunt the orangutans to eat them.

The animals have been protected from hunting by the Indonesian government since 1930. Orangutans are still being hunted as food in some areas, however. They are also captured to be kept as status symbols, signs of their owners' wealth and importance. Another serious threat comes from the shooting of orangutan mothers so that their infants can be sold as pets.

The overall orangutan population has declined by 90 percent in the past century, according to the WWF. The Orangutan Conservancy estimates that there are now about 40,000 orangutans living on Borneo and Sumatra. If the current rate of population decline continues, the conservancy predicts that orangutans will be extinct in nature within the next 25 years.

More than half of orangutans live outside protected areas.

Saving the Orangutan

In the rainforests of Indonesia and Malaysia, some people see natural beauty, while others see an opportunity to log trees and make money, often illegally. A rainforest develops over many years into a dense collection of trees and other plants. The rainforest is a rich habitat suitable for orangutans and many other living things. With power saws and moving equipment, however, loggers can cut down trees and flatten land quickly.

Some rainforest areas have been set aside by governments as national parks or reserves. In these areas, logging and farming are often not permitted, but illegal logging is occurring anyway. Hiring more guards to patrol protected areas is one way to reduce illegal logging and save some of the trees.

An even greater threat to rainforests, however, comes from industrial farming outside protected areas. The creation of one large palm oil plantation can destroy almost 80 square miles (more than 200 sq. km) of forest. As worldwide demand for palm oil has increased, people have taken over more of the rainforests to build large palm oil plantations.

To clear land quickly, people often burn an area of the forest. Then, the remaining forest near the cleared area receives more sunlight than it used to. Dense, humid forest areas dry out from the heat of the Sun. Naturally occurring fires are becoming worse as a result. These fires destroy even more forest. Some burning even travels underground, through the upper layer of soil that contains plant matter. A fire can then spread from one forested area to another.

In Indonesia, large fires in 1997 and 1998 burned more than 7,800 square miles (20,200 sq. km) of forest. Some of these fires were the result of drought. Many others were set on purpose or were caused by clearing land and exposing forests to more sunlight. Thousands of animals died in these fires, including at least 1,000 to 2,000 orangutans. Thousands more were injured or left with no natural habitat in which to live.

To save the rainforests, and the orangutans that live there, some people are working to make sure that palm oil plantations are established in areas of open grassland rather than in rainforest areas. Various groups are placing pressure on local governments to better regulate use of the land. Around the world, people are learning to ask for products made with palm oil from plants raised by methods that preserve the environment.

The greatest population decline for orangutans has occurred in recent decades.

Back from the Brink

Orangutan Foundation International (OFI) was started in 1986. The mission of the foundation is to support conservation and understanding of the orangutan and its rainforest habitat. In order to do this, the OFI cares for and **rehabilitates** orangutans that have been rescued from the pet trade. As many of these rescued animals as possible are returned to the forest. For those who cannot return to the forest, the OFI provides a sanctuary, or protected area, in which the apes can live.

The OFI makes people aware of orangutans as unique and valuable creatures. The foundation has made both the public and governments aware of threats to orangutans and to rainforests. It has developed education packages about orangutans for schoolchildren in Indonesia. The OFI also works to stop illegal logging and forest destruction. This and other organizations are working to save the orangutans of Asia. For more information on the status of orangutans, contact:

Orangutan Foundation International
822 South Wellesley Avenue
Los Angeles, CA 90049

Many groups are working to save large areas of forest where the remaining orangutans may be able to survive.

Activity

Debating helps people think about ideas thoughtfully and carefully. When people debate, two sides take a different viewpoint on a subject. Each side takes turns presenting arguments to support its view.

Use the Take a Stand sections found throughout this book as a starting point for debate topics. Organize your friends or classmates into two teams. One team will argue in favor of the topic, and the other will argue against. Each team should research the issue thoroughly using reliable sources of information, including books, scientific journals, and trustworthy websites. Take notes of important facts that support your side of the debate. Prepare your argument using these facts to support your opinion.

During the debate, the members of each team are given a set amount of time to make their arguments. The team arguing the For side goes first. They have five minutes to present their case. All members of the team should participate equally. Then, the team arguing the Against side presents its arguments. Each team should take notes of the main points the other team argues.

After both teams have made their arguments, they get three minutes to prepare their rebuttals. Teams review their notes from the previous round. The teams focus on trying to disprove each of the main points made by the other team using solid facts. Each team gets three minutes to make its rebuttal. The team arguing the Against side goes first. Students and teachers watching the debate serve as judges. They should try to judge the debate fairly using a standard score sheet, such as the example below.

Criteria	Rate: 1-10	Sample Comments
1. Were the arguments well organized?	8	logical arguments, easy to follow
2. Did team members participate equally?	9	divided time evenly between members
3. Did team members speak loudly and clearly?	3	some members were difficult to hear
4. Were rebuttals specific to the other team's arguments?	6	rebuttals were specific, more facts needed
5. Was respect shown for the other team?	10	all members showed respect to the other team

Quiz

1. What are the four types of great apes?

2. Name the two islands orangutans live on.

3. In what kind of structure are baby orangutans born?

5. What body part makes the orangutan's long call louder?

6. Which teeth do orangutans display to scare their competitors?

4. What is the main reason male orangutans live and travel alone?

8. Besides natural disasters, what causes the rainforest habitat to decrease?

10. The area in which an orangutan travels in search of food is called what?

7. Besides learning from their mothers, how do young orangutans learn the skills they need to survive?

9. In the past century, orangutans decreased by what percentage?

Answers:
1. orangutans, chimpanzees, bonobos, and gorillas 2. Borneo and Sumatra 3. a nest 4. This makes it easier for them to find food and survive. 5. the animal's throat pouch 6. canine teeth 7. by playing with one another. 8. human development 9. 90 percent 10. its home range

     Animals on the Brink

Key Words

arboreal: living in or among trees

canine: one of four pointed teeth near the front of mouth

diurnal: active during the day

DNA: biological molecule that gives living things their special features

dominance hierarchy: regular, predictable dominance relationships in a group

dominant: controlling

ecosystems: communities of living things and resources

endangered: in danger of no longer surviving in the world

extinct: no longer surviving in the world

food web: connecting food chains that show how energy flows from one organism to another through diet

genetic makeup: the pattern of genes, the building blocks for all living things

gestation period: the length of time that a female is pregnant with young

home range: the entire area in which an animal lives

mammals: warm-blooded animals that have hair or fur and nurse their young

order: one of eight major ranks used to classify animals, between class and family

organisms: forms of life

predators: animals that live by hunting other animals for food

prehensile: specially adapted for gripping objects

primates: the large category of animals that includes apes, humans, monkeys, and prosimians

rehabilitates: restores to a normal state of physical or mental health

species: group of individuals with common characteristics

vertebrate: having a backbone that can bend

weaned: when an animal no longer drinks milk from its mother

Index

arm 7, 11, 26

birth 19, 20, 23, 40
body language 16
bonobos 8
Borneo 4, 7, 19, 27, 29, 38, 41, 46

cheek 23, 34, 35
classification 7, 8
communication 15
competition 35, 36

Dayak 38
development 23
dominance 15, 35

feet 7, 11, 18, 20, 22, 23, 24
folklore 38
food 12, 13, 17, 19, 20, 23, 24, 25, 27, 28, 29, 30, 31, 32, 36, 38, 41, 46

gorillas 8

habitat 24, 27, 28, 29, 33, 35, 39, 40, 41, 42, 44, 46
hair 4, 7, 9, 20, 22, 38,
hand 7, 10, 11, 20, 22, 24, 39
home range 23, 27

logging 37, 42, 44

mating 19, 23
monkeys 8

nests 10, 18 19, 20, 23, 30

pet 17, 44
play 13, 15, 22, 23, 33, 35
population 23, 41, 43
prosimians 8

rainforest 4, 7, 8, 10, 13, 22, 24, 28, 29, 33, 35, 36, 38, 42, 44, 46

size 8, 27, 30, 36
skin 9, 10, 20, 34
Sumatra 4, 7, 27, 28, 29, 35, 41

tree 6, 10, 11, 13, 16, 17, 18, 20, 22, 23, 24, 26, 27, 28, 29, 30, 33, 35, 36, 39, 41, 42

weight 7, 26

young 4, 13, 15, 16, 17, 19, 20, 22, 23, 30, 32, 33, 34, 35, 37, 38, 46

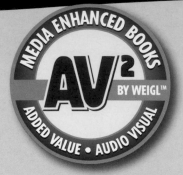

Log on to www.av2books.com

AV² by Weigl brings you media enhanced books that support active learning. Go to www.av2books.com, and enter the special code found on page 2 of this book. You will gain access to enriched and enhanced content that supplements and complements this book. Content includes video, audio, weblinks, quizzes, a slide show, and activities.

AV² Online Navigation

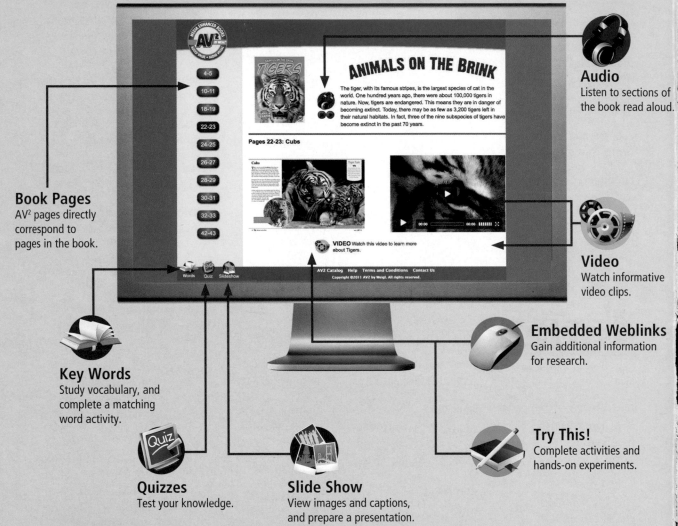

Book Pages
AV² pages directly correspond to pages in the book.

Key Words
Study vocabulary, and complete a matching word activity.

Quizzes
Test your knowledge.

Slide Show
View images and captions, and prepare a presentation.

Audio
Listen to sections of the book read aloud.

Video
Watch informative video clips.

Embedded Weblinks
Gain additional information for research.

Try This!
Complete activities and hands-on experiments.

AV² was built to bridge the gap between print and digital. We encourage you to tell us what you like and what you want to see in the future.

Sign up to be an AV² Ambassador at www.av2books.com/ambassador.

Due to the dynamic nature of the Internet, some of the URLs and activities provided as part of AV² by Weigl may have changed or ceased to exist. AV² by Weigl accepts no responsibility for any such changes. All media enhanced books are regularly monitored to update addresses and sites in a timely manner. Contact AV² by Weigl at 1-866-649-3445 or av2books@weigl.com with any questions, comments, or feedback.